CELEBRATING THE NAME ERIC

Celebrating the Name Eric

Walter the Educator

Silent King Books

Copyright © 2024 by Walter the Educator

All rights reserved. No part of this book may be reproduced in any manner whatsoever without written permission except in the case of brief quotations embodied in critical articles and reviews.

First Printing, 2024

Disclaimer
This book is a literary work; poems are not about specific persons, locations, situations, and/or circumstances unless mentioned in a historical context. This book is for entertainment and informational purposes only. The author and publisher offer this information without warranties expressed or implied. No matter the grounds, neither the author nor the publisher will be accountable for any losses, injuries, or other damages caused by the reader's use of this book. The use of this book acknowledges an understanding and acceptance of this disclaimer.

dedicated to everyone with the first name of Eric

ERIC

In realms of stars where dreams entwine,

ERIC

A name emerges, bold and fine,

ERIC

Eric, a beacon in the night,

ERIC

In whispered winds, his essence alight.

ERIC

Through ancient woods, his footsteps tread,

ERIC

A path of destiny, widely spread,

ERIC

With every beat, his heart does soar,

ERIC

A symphony of dreams he'll explore.

ERIC

In twilight's dance, his spirit roams,

ERIC

Among the whispers and honeycombs,

ERIC

Eric, the seeker, brave and true,

ERIC

In realms of wonder, he'll pursue.

ERIC

Beneath the moon's enchanted glow,

ERIC

Eric wanders, with purpose to know,

ERIC

Each shadow cast, a tale untold,

ERIC

In mystic realms, his secrets unfold.

ERIC

Through fields of gold and azure skies,

ERIC

Eric's laughter, a sweet surprise,

ERIC

In every echo, his name resounds,

ERIC

A melody in nature's bounds.

ERIC

In gardens where the roses weep,

ERIC

Eric finds solace, secrets to keep,

ERIC

With gentle hands, he tends the earth,

ERIC

Breathing life into every birth.

ERIC

In oceans deep, where mysteries lie,

ERIC

Eric dives, with a fearless cry,

ERIC

Among the coral, he finds his peace,

ERIC

In the embrace of the great cerulean seas.

ERIC

In bustling streets, where chaos reigns,

ERIC

Eric stands tall, unbound by chains,

ERIC

With words of wisdom, he'll guide the lost,

ERIC

A beacon of hope, no matter the cost.

ERIC

In fireside tales, his legend grows,

ERIC

Eric, the hero, whom everyone knows,

ERIC

With courage burning in his eyes,

ERIC

He'll face the darkness, unafraid to rise.

ERIC

In the tapestry of life, his thread weaves,

ERIC

Eric, the dreamer, who never leaves,

ERIC

With every step, he paints his story,

ERIC

In shades of glory, eternal and free.

ERIC

ABOUT THE CREATOR

Walter the Educator is one of the pseudonyms for Walter Anderson. Formally educated in Chemistry, Business, and Education, he is an educator, an author, a diverse entrepreneur, and he is the son of a disabled war veteran. "Walter the Educator" shares his time between educating and creating. He holds interests and owns several creative projects that entertain, enlighten, enhance, and educate, hoping to inspire and motivate you.

Follow, find new works, and stay up to date
with Walter the Educator™
at WaltertheEducator.com

www.ingramcontent.com/pod-product-compliance
Lightning Source LLC
LaVergne TN
LVHW052009060526
838201LV00059B/3939